D0591287

FAVOURITE
CHRISTMAS SONGS
& STORIES

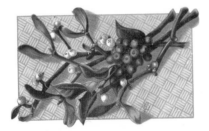

FAVOURITE CHRISTMAS SONGS & STORIES

Michael O'Mara Books Limited

First published in Great Britain in 1997 by
Michael O'Mara Books Limited
9 Lion Yard, Tremadoc Road
London SW4 7NQ

Copyright © 1997 by Michael O'Mara Books Limited

All rights reserved. No part of this publication may be reproduced, stored in a retrieval
system, or transmitted by any means, without the prior permission in writing of the
publisher, nor be otherwise circulated in any form of binding or cover other than that
in which it is published and without a similar condition including this condition being
imposed on the subsequent purchaser.

The publisher would like to thank Brenda and Gareth Davis for their help in
researching illustrative material

A CIP catalogue record for this book is available from the British Library

ISBN 1-85479-328-4

1 3 5 7 9 10 8 6 4 2

Designed by Mick Keates
Typeset by Concise Artisans

Printed in Great Britain by
Butler & Tanner Limited

Contents

Quotations	7–8	The Little Match Girl		
Little Women LOUISA M. ALCOTT	9	HANS CHRISTIAN ANDERSEN	28	
The First Christmas Card	10	The Oxen THOMAS HARDY	29	
The Post Office	11	Carolling	30	
Baboushka	12	Old Christmas WASHINGTON IRVING	31	
The Wise Men MATTHEW 2:11-12	14	The Twelve Days of Christmas	32	
'What Can I Give Him?' CHRISTINA ROSSETTI	15	December 25th	35	
A Visit from St. Nicholas CLEMENT C. MOORE	16	Stories about Cats MRS SURR	36	
The Thieves Who Couldn't Help Sneezing		The Mistletoe CLINTON SCOLLARD	37	
THOMAS HARDY	17	A Christmas Carol CHARLES DICKENS	38	
Father Christmas Around the World	18	Little Jack Horner HENRY CAREY	39	
A Child's Christmas in Wales DYLAN THOMAS	20	Wassail	40	
Christmas proverbs	21	Wassail Bowl	41	
The Fir-Tree HANS CHRISTIAN ANDERSEN	22	Gloucestershire Carol	42	
The Christmas Tree		Old Christmas WASHINGTON IRVING	43	
DICTIONARY OF DAILY WANTS	23	Christmas Bells		
'Christmas even in the Olden Time'		HENRY WADSWORTH LONGFELLOW	44	
SIR WALTER SCOTT	24	Recipie for roast turkey ELIZA ACTON	45	
Christmas Greeting from a Fairy to a Child		Boxing Day	46	
LEWIS CARROLL	25	Pickwick Papers CHARLES DICKENS	47	
Extract from Reader's Digest	26	Winter ALFRED LORD TENNYSON	48	
Christmas is Coming MOTHER GOOSE	27			

At Christmas play and make good cheer,
For Christmas comes but once a year.

THOMAS TUSSER, ENGLISH FARMER,
FIVE HUNDRED POINTS OF GOOD HUSBANDRY

I have often thought, says Sir Roger, it happens
very well that Christmas should fall out in the
Middle of Winter

JOSEPH ADDISON, *THE SPECTATOR, 269*

At Christmas I no more desire a rose
Than wish a snow in May's newfangled mirth.

WILLIAM SHAKESPEARE, *LOVE'S LABOUR'S LOST I:1*

LITTLE WOMEN

LOUISA M. ALCOTT

On Christmas night, a dozen girls piled on to the bed, which was the dress-circle, and sat before the blue and yellow chintz curtains in a most flattering state of expectancy. There was a good deal of rustling and whispering behind the curtain, a trifle of lamp-smoke, and an occasional giggle from Amy who was apt to get hysterical in the excitement of the moment. Presently a bell sounded, the curtains flew apart, and the Operatic Tragedy began.

THE FIRST CHRISTMAS CARD

Today Christmas cards clog up the postal system in an enormous deluge every year, however it was only in December 1843 that the first Christmas card was sent.

Sir Henry Cole, a British aristocrat, commissioned a painter, John Calcott Horsley, to design a card to send to his family and friends. He wanted something new to send instead of his usual Christmas letter.

The resulting card showed a scene of a family drinking a toast to the Christmas season. It was a hand-coloured lithograph and was sold by its publisher – a London printer – at 1 shilling a time. 1,000 copies were sold and the idea took hold and spread until it reached the enormous level of industry it is today.

THE POST OFFICE

By 1900, the Christmas card business had expanded to such a level that the Post Office sometimes had trouble handling all the mail. As everyone wanted their card to arrive on Christmas Eve or Christmas Day, they would only mail them at the very last minute. To try to overcome this problem, the Post Office issued a special postmark:

POSTED IN ADVANCE
FOR DELIVERY ON
CHRISTMAS DAY

Those cards displaying this postmark were retained in the local sorting office until Christmas morning when they would all be delivered at once to the household.

BABOUSHKA

Once upon a time, living deep in the forest, there was an old woman called Baboushka. All day she cleaned, cooked, sewed and gathered wood, singing songs to keep herself company, and she was never lonely.

One day in the middle of winter, she heard voices coming towards her house through the trees. Baboushka excitedly ran into the house to put the kettle on the hob. She had just laid out more logs for the fire when there was a knock on the door.

When she had lifted her heavy old wooden latch and swung open the door, she was confronted with three weary travellers.

'We have lost our way in the forest,' said one, 'and it is growing dark outside. Might we shelter here and rest a little before going on our way?'

'Of course, of course,' Baboushka exclaimed. 'Come in and warm yourselves.'

One by one the three travellers came in, shaking the snow from their fine clothes. As they sat around the fire drinking tea and eating bread, Baboushka asked them where they were going.

'We are searching for the baby prince,' said the youngest of the three. 'His star has guided us so far, but now the sky is full of snow and we can't see it anymore.'

'Don't worry,' said Baboushka, 'I'll show you where the road is.'

'Only the star can lead us to the Christ child,' he replied, and he showed her the rich presents they were taking to give to the child when they found him.

Baboushka's eyes grew wide. 'I wish I could see this child,' she murmured.

'Come with us,' the three travellers cried. 'Help us in our search.'

But Baboushka declined saying, 'No. I'm much too old to travel.'

When the three had gone on their way, Baboushka sat in her rocking chair and pondered on the visit. Suddenly she jumped to her feet.

'I will go and join the search. I'll go tomorrow.' She quickly packed up all her greatest treasures to take as presents – a wooden horse, an old doll, a cloth ball, some painted fir cones and some pretty feathers – and early the next morning set off in the snow.

But she never found the three kings, the bright star or the baby prince, and everyone she asked laughed and mocked at her questions. No one could help her.

To this day, Baboushka has never stopped searching for the baby prince. And whenever she meets a child who is ill or unhappy, she digs into her bag and always finds some little toy to make them smile.

TRADITIONAL RUSSIAN TALE

RAPHAEL TUCK & SONS   LONDON

THE WISE MEN

And when they were come into the house,
They saw the young child with Mary his mother,
and fell down, and worshipped him:
and when they had opened their treasures,
*   they presented unto him gifts; gold,*
*   and frankincense, and myrrh.*
*   And being warned of God in a*
*   dream that they should not return to*
*   Herod, they departed into their own*
*   country another way.*

Matthew 2:11-12

Variously known as the Three Kings, the Three Wise Men or the Magi, they are generally accepted as being integral to the story of the Nativity. In fact they only appear in St. Matthew's Gospel and estimates of their number have varied: St. Augustine believed there had been 12 Wise Men.

In the second century, the Pope decreed that there were to be three, because, according to St. Matthew, three gifts were presented to Jesus — gold, frankincense and myrrh.

What can I give Him,
Poor as I am?
If I were a shepherd
I would bring a lamb;
If I were a wise man
I would do my part;
Yet what I can I give Him –
Give my heart.

From *In the Bleak Midwinter*
Christina Rossetti

A Visit from St. Nicholas

Clement C. Moore

'Twas the night before Christmas, when all through the house
Not a creature was stirring, not even a mouse;
The stockings were hung by the chimney with care,
In hopes that St. Nicholas soon would be there;
The children were nestled all snug in their beds,
While visions of sugar-plums danced in their heads;
And Mamma in her kerchief, and I in my cap,
Had just settled our brains for a long winter's nap,
When out on the lawn there arose such a clatter,
I sprang from the bed to see what was the matter.
Away to the window I flew like a flash,
Tore open the shutters and threw up the sash.
The moon on the breast of the newfallen snow
Gave the lustre of mid-day to objects below,
When what to my wondering eyes should appear,
But a miniature sleigh and eight tiny reindeer,
With a little old driver, so lively and quick,
I knew in a moment it must be St. Nick.

Many years ago, when oak trees now past their prime were about as large as elderly gentlemen's walking-sticks, there lived in Wessex a yeoman's son, whose name was Hubert. He was about fourteen years of age, and was as remarkable for his candour and lightness of heart as for his physical courage, of which, indeed, he was a little vain.

One cold Christmas Eve his father, having no other help at hand, sent him on an important errand to a small town several miles from home. He travelled on horseback, and was detained by the business till a late hour of the evening. At last, however, it was completed; he returned to the inn, the horse was saddled, and he started on his way. His journey homeward lay through the Vale of Blackmore, a fertile but somewhat lonely district, with heavy clay roads and crooked lanes. In those days, too, a great part of it was thickly wooded.

It must have been about nine o'clock when, riding along amid the overhanging trees upon his stout-legged cob, Jerry, and singing a Christmas carol, to be in harmony with the season, Hubert fancied that he heard a noise among the boughs.

The Thieves who Couldn't Help Sneezing Thomas Hardy

FATHER CHRISTMAS AROUND THE WORLD

In GREAT BRITAIN Father Christmas delivers presents to the children on Christmas Eve. In AMERICA Santa Claus visits the children, but other countries have very different gift-givers:

IN FRANCE, baby Jesus is usually the gift-giver, but in some areas Tante Aria (Mother Air), riding a donkey and accompanied by Father Star, delivers the presents.

IN GERMANY they are visited by Weihnachtsman, who carries a large sack of presents and carries a bundle of sticks in one hand and a Christmas tree in the other.

IN ITALY Befana, known in RUSSIA as Baboushka, is an old woman who has been looking for the Christ Child ever since He was born to give Him her presents. She flies through the air and leaves a gift for every child she passes.

IN SPAIN presents are delivered by the Wise Men on the date of Epiphany on 6th January. Epiphany is a Greek word meaning 'manifestation', when Christ manifested himself to the Gentiles – the Three Kings who had come to worship Him.

IN THE NETHERLANDS Sinterklass, dressed in bishop's robes, gives out the presents to good children while his helper, Swarte Piet (Black Peter), dressed in black, carries switches for bad boys and girls.

IN CZECHOSLOVAKIA, Svaty Mikulas arrives at Chritmas time with an angel and an evil spirit.

IN SOME MIDDLE-EASTERN COUNTRIES, the Gentle Camel – the youngest of the three camels who carried the Wise Men – gives out all the gifts.

A CHILD'S CHRISTMAS
IN WALES

DYLAN THOMAS

No, no, no, in the bat-black, snow-white belfries, tugged
by bishops and storks. And they rang their tidings over
the bandaged town, over the frozen foam of the powder and
ice-cream hills, over the crackling sea. It seemed that all the
churches boomed for joy under my window; and the weather-
cocks crew for Christmas, on our fence.

CHRISTMAS PROVERBS

As many mince pies as you taste at Christmas,
so many happy months you will have.

DENHAM TRACTS, II

If Christmas day on a Sunday fall,
A troublous winter we shall have all.

DENHAM PROVERBS, 63

If Christmas day on Monday be,
A wintry winter you shall see.

DENHAM PROVERBS, 70

THE FIR-TREE

HANS CHRISTIAN ANDERSEN

The fir-tree was placed in a great tub filled with sand, but no one could see that it was a tub, for it was all hung with greenery and stood on a gay carpet. How the tree trembled! What was coming now? The young ladies and the servants decked it out. On its branches they hung little nets cut out of coloured paper, each full of sugarplums; gilt apples and nuts hung down as if they were growing, and over a hundred red, blue, and white tapers were fastened among the branches. Dolls as life-like as human beings – the fir-tree had never seen any before – were suspended among the green, and right up at the top was fixed a gold tinsel star; it was gorgeous, quite unusually gorgeous!

THE CHRISTMAS TREE

The custom of having illuminated trees at Christmas, laden with pretty little trifles, as momentoes to be presented to the guests of the Christmas party, is derived from Germany. A young fir is generally selected for the Christmas Tree, and little presents of various kinds are bound on the branches, as, crochet-purses, bonbons, preserved fruits, alum-baskets, charms, dolls, toys in endless variety etc., distributed over the tree according to fancy. The whole is illuminated by numerous little wax tapers, which are lighted just before the guests are admitted to inspect the tree. Before the tapers are quite burnt out the guests all assemble around the tree, and the souvenirs are taken off and presented to the guests whose names have either been previously appended to them, or at the discretion of the distributor.

THE DICTIONARY OF DAILY WANTS, 1858

'CHRISTMAS EVEN IN THE OLDEN TIME'

SIR WALTER SCOTT

And well our Christian sires of old
Loved when the year its course had roll'd,
And brought blithe Christmas back again,
With all his hospitable train.
Domestic and religious rite
Gave honour to that holy night.

CHRISTMAS GREETING FROM A FAIRY TO A CHILD

LEWIS CARROLL

Lady, dear, if Fairies may
    For a moment lay aside
Cunning tricks and elfish play,
    'Tis at happy Christmas-tide

We have heard the children say –
    Gentle children, whom we love –
Long ago on Christmas Day,
    Came a message from above.

Still, as Christmas-tide comes round,
    They remember it again –
Echo still the joyful sound
    'Peace on earth, good-will to men!'

Yet the hearts must childlike be
    Where such heavenly guests abide;
Unto children, in their glee,
    All the year is Christmas-tide!

Thus, forgetting tricks and play
    For a moment, Lady dear,
We would wish you, if we may,
    Merry Christmas, glad New Year!

Health, Peace, and sweet content be yours.
Shakespeare

After the Sunday school class had sung 'Silent Night' and been told the Christmas story, the teacher suggested that her pupils draw the Nativity scene. A little boy finished first. The teacher praised his drawing of the manger, of Joseph, of Mary and the infant. But she was puzzled by a roly-poly figure off to one side and asked who it was. 'Oh,' explained the youngster, 'that's Round John Virgin'.

READER'S DIGEST, DECEMBER 1958

CHRISTMAS IS COMING

MOTHER GOOSE

Christmas is coming, the geese are getting fat,
Please to put a penny in an old man's hat;
If you haven't got a penny a ha'penny will do,
If you haven't got a ha'penny, God bless you.

THE LITTLE MATCH GIRL

HANS CHRISTIAN ANDERSEN

Her hands were almost dead with cold. Ah! One little match might do her good! If she dared take only one out of the box, strike it on the wall, and warm her fingers! She took one out and struck it. How it sputtered and burned!

It was a warm, bright flame, like a little candle, when she held her hands over it. It was a wonderful little light, and it really seemed to the child as though she were sitting in front of a great iron stove with polished brass feet and brass ornaments. How the fire burned, and how it warmed! But what was that? The little girl was already stretching out her feet to warm them too, when – out went the little flame, the stove vanished, and she had only the remains of the burned match in her hand.

She struck a second one on the wall; it burned and gave a light, and where the light fell on the wall it became transparent, like a veil – she could see right into the room. A white tablecloth was spread upon the table, which was decked with shining china dishes, and there was a lovely smell of roast goose stuffed with apples and prunes. What pleased the poor little girl more than anything was that the goose hopped down from the dish and came waddling across the floor straight towards her. Just at that moment, out went the match, and only the thick, cold wall was to be seen. So she lighted another match. And there she was sitting under the beautiful Christmas tree; it was much larger and more decorated than the one she had seen through the glass doors at the rich merchant's. The green boughs were lit up with thousands of candles, and gaily painted figures, like those in the shop windows, looked down on her. The little girl stretched her hands out towards them and – out went the match. The Christmas candles rose higher and higher, till they were only the stars in the sky; one of them fell, leaving a long fiery trail behind it.

THE OXEN

THOMAS HARDY

Christmas Eve, and twelve of the clock.
'Now they are all on their knees,'
An elder said as we sat in a flock
By the embers in hearthside ease.

We pictured the meek mild creatures where
They dwelt in their straw pen,
Nor did it occur to one of us there
To doubt they were kneeling then.

So fair a fancy few would weave
In these years! Yet, I feel
If someone said on Christmas Eve,
'Come; see the oxen kneel

'In the lonely barton by yonder coomb,
Our childhood used to know,'
I should go with him in the gloom,
Hoping it might be so.

CAROLLING

Originally the word 'carol' is said to derive from the Greek word 'choraulein' which was actually a dance accompanied by the flute ('choros' means dance and 'aulein' to play the flute). In medieval times a 'carol' meant a dance in a circle accompanied with singing. The dancers were usually girls.

Nowadays the word has changed to refer to the song alone.

OLD CHRISTMAS

WASHINGTON IRVING

In the course of a December tour in Yorkshire, I rode for a long distance in one of the public coaches, on the day preceding Christmas. The coach was crowded, both inside and out, with passengers, who, by their talk, seemed principally bound to the mansions of relatives or friends to eat the Christmas Dinner. It was loaded also with hampers of game, and baskets and boxes of delicacies.

THE TWELVE DAYS OF CHRISTMAS

The first day of Christmas
My true love sent to me
A partridge in a pear tree.

The second day of Christmas
My true love sent to me
Two turtle doves, and
A partridge in a pear tree.

The third day of Christmas
My true love sent to me
Three French hens,
Two turtle doves, and
A partridge in a pear tree.

The fourth day of Christmas
My true love sent to me
Four colly birds,
Three French hens,
Two turtle doves, and
A partridge in a pear tree.

The fifth day of Christmas
My true love sent to me
Five gold rings,
Four colly birds,
Three French hens,
Two turtle doves, and
A partridge in a pear tree.

The sixth day of Christmas
My true love sent to me
Six geese a-laying,
Five gold rings,
Four colly birds,
Three French hens,
Two turtle doves, and
A partridge in a pear tree.

The seventh day of Christmas
My true love sent to me
Seven swans a-swimming,
Six geese a-laying,
Five gold rings,
Four colly birds,
Three French hens,
Two turtle doves, and
A partridge in a pear tree.

The ninth day of Christmas
My true love sent to me
Nine drummers drumming,
Eight maids a-milking,
Seven swans a-swimming,
Six geese a-laying,
Five gold rings,
Four colly birds,
Three French hens,
Two turtle doves, and
A partridge in a pear tree.

The eighth day of Christmas
My true love sent to me
Eight maids a-milking,
Seven swans a-swimming,
Six geese a-laying,
Five gold rings,
Four colly birds,
Three French hens,
Two turtle doves, and
A partridge in a pear tree.

The tenth day of Christmas
My true love sent to me
Ten pipers piping,
Nine drummers drumming,
Eight maids a-milking,
Seven swans a-swimming,
Six geese a-laying,
Five gold rings,
Four colly birds,
Three French hens,
Two turtle doves, and
A partridge in a pear tree.

The eleventh day of Christmas
My true love sent to me
Eleven ladies dancing,
Ten pipers piping,
Nine drummers drumming,
Eight maids a-milking,
Seven swans a-swimming,
Six geese a-laying,
Five gold rings,
Four colly birds,
Three French hens,
Two turtle doves, and
A partridge in a pear tree.

The twelfth day of Christmas
My true love sent to me
Twelve lords a-leaping,
Eleven ladies dancing,
Ten pipers piping,
Nine drummers drumming,
Eight maids a-milking,
Seven swans a-swimming,
Six geese a-laying,
Five gold rings,
Four colly birds,
Three French hens,
Two turtle doves, and
A partridge in a pear tree.

December 25th

No particular date was celebrated for the exact day of Christ's birth in the early days of Christianity. Four dates were particularly popular – 1 January, 6 January, 25 March or 20 May. The latter was the most celebrated as it was considered that, as it fell in spring with lambs out in the fields, it was the most accurate time for shepherds to be out in the fields tending their flocks, and so in place to receive the great tidings from the angels.

In the fourth century, during Roman times, the birthday of the sun god Mithras was observed on 25 December. This was celebrated under the religion of Mithraism. On that date they held feasts and celebrated the old pagan rites of the Saturnalia. Fortunately for the Christians, as that date was declared a special day of Nativity, they were allowed to honour it with a Mass. Christ's Mass therefore became Christmas with all the feasting and fun stemming from the pagan celebrations.

When we sit 'curtained and closed, and warm'
around the Christmas log-piled fire, incomplete
indeed is our happy family circle if puss is not on the
rug at its centre. Our playmate she has been from
earliest childhood and vainly may memory seek to
recall the house of our first introduction to the cat.

MRS SURR, *STORIES ABOUT CATS*, 1882

THE MISTLETOE

CLINTON SCOLLARD

It was after the maze and mirth of the
    dance,
Where a spray of green mistletoe swayed,
That I met – and I vow that the meeting was
    chance! –
With a very adorable maid.

I stood for a moment in tremor of doubt,
Then kissed her, half looking for war:
But – 'Why did you wait, Sir!' she said,
    with a pout,
'Pray, what is the mistletoe for?'

A Christmas Carol

Charles Dickens

Oh, a wonderful pudding! Bob Cratchit said, and calmly too, that he regarded it as the greatest success achieved by Mrs. Cratchit since their marriage. Mrs. Cratchit said that now the weight was off her mind, she would confess she had had her doubts about the quantity of flour. Everybody had something to say about it, but nobody said or thought it was at all a small pudding for a large family. It would have been flat heresy to do so. Any Cratchit would have blushed to hint at such a thing.

At last the dinner was all done, the cloth was cleared, the hearth swept, and the fire made up. The compound in the jug being tasted, and considered perfect, apples and oranges were put upon the table, and a shovel-full of chestnuts on the fire. Then all the Cratchit family drew round the hearth, in what Bob Cratchit called a circle, meaning half a one; and at Bob Cratchit's elbow stood the family display of glass. Two tumblers, and a custard-cup without a handle.

These held the hot stuff from the jug, however, as well as golden goblets would have done; and Bob served it out with beaming looks, while the chestnuts on the fire sputtered and cracked noisily. Then Bob proposed:

'A Merry Christmas to us all, my dears. God bless us!'

Which all the family re-echoed.

'God bless us every one!' said Tiny Tim, the last of all.

LITTLE
JACK HORNER

Little Jack Horner
Sat in a corner
Eating a Christmas pie;
He put in his thumb
And pulled out a plum,
And said, What a good boy am I!

HENRY CAREY, *NAMBY PAMBY*

WASSAIL

Wassail stems from the word 'wes', meaning 'be in good health'. It was a drink of particular potency invented in Anglo-Saxon times and consisted of pieces of bread floating on spiced ale. Each wassailer would fish out a piece of the bread known as a 'toast' and, as he swallowed it, would give good wishes to another member of the circle.

Those who were not included in the circle could go a-wassailing – begging for money to buy a bowl of wassail.

WASSAIL BOWL

6 pints brown ale
½ pound soft brown sugar
(or ½–1 cup US coffee sugar)
1 large cinnamon stick
½ teaspoon ground ginger

2 roasted apples
1 teaspoon grated nutmeg

2 thinly sliced lemons
1 bottle inexpensive amontillado sherry

Pour 2 pints of ale into a large saucepan, together with the sugar and cinnamon stick. Heat gently until the sugar has dissolved before adding all the other ingredients. Gradually bring the mixture to the boil. To impart an extra kick, add a glass of brandy just before serving. Serves 25-30.

Wassail, Wassail, all over the town!
Our toast is white, and our ale
is brown,
Our bowl it is made of the white
maple tree:
With the wassailing bowl we'll
drink to thee.

So here is to Cherry and to his
right cheek,
Pray God send our master a good
piece of beef,
And a good piece of beef that may
we all see;
With the wassailing bowl we'll
drink to thee.

FROM A TRADITIONAL GLOUCESTERSHIRE
CAROL

OLD CHRISTMAS AND BRACEBRIDGE HALL

WASHINGTON IRVING

The old gentleman's whole countenance beamed with a serene look of indwelling delight, as he stirred this mighty bowl. Having raised it to his lips, with a hearty wish of a merry Christmas to all present, he sent it brimming round the board, for every one to follow his example, according to the primitive style; pronouncing it 'the ancient fountain of good feeling, where all hearts met together'.

There was much laughing and rallying as the honest emblem of Christmas joviality circulated, and was kissed rather coyly by the ladies. When it reached Master Simon he raised it in both hands, and with the air of a boon companion struck up an old Wassail chanson:

> The browne bowle,
> The merry browne bowle,
> As it goes round about-a,
>   Fill
>   Still,
> Let the world say what it will,
> And drink your fill all out-a.
>
> The deep canne,
> The merry deep canne,
> As thou dost freely quaff-a,
>   Sing,
>   Fling,
> Be as merry as a king,
> And sound a lusty laugh-a.

CHRISTMAS BELLS

HENRY WADSWORTH LONGFELLOW

I heard the bells on Christmas day
Their old familiar carols play,
   And wild and sweet
   The words repeat
Of 'Peace on earth, good will to men!'

Turkey

It is thought that the name for this bird originally came from Portuguese explorers. They gave the name to guineafowl brought from New Guinea while they were travelling through Turkey.

Recipie for roast Turkey

In very cold weather a turkey in its feathers will hang (in an airy larder) quite a fortnight with advantage; and however fine a quality of bird it may be, unless sufficiently long kept, it will prove not worth the dressing, though it should always be perfectly sweet when prepared for the table. Pluck, draw and singe it with exceeding care; wash, and then dry it thoroughly with clean cloths, or merely wipe the outside well, without wetting it, and pour water plentifully through the inside. Fill the breast with forcemeat, or with the finest sausagemeat, highly seasoned with minced herbs, lemon rind, mace, and cayenne. Truss the bird firmly, lay it to a clear sound fire, baste it constantly and bountifully with butter, and serve it when done with good brown gravy, and well-made bread sauce. An entire chain of delicate fried sausages is still often placed in the dish round a turkey as garnish.

ELIZA ACTON, *MODERN COOKERY FOR PRIVATE FAMILIES* (1880s)

BOXING DAY

Boxing Day – December 26 – has nothing to do with the sport. It originally comes from a medieval custom: on the day after Christmas church collection boxes were emptied and the proceeds were distributed among the poor of the parish.

Later a custom developed of giving servants tips and presents, known as 'Christmas boxes' on this day.

PICKWICK PAPERS

CHARLES DICKENS

Mr. Winkle, stooping forward with his body half doubled up, was being assisted over the ice by Mr. Weller, in a very singular and un-swanlike manner, when Mr. Pickwick most innocently shouted from the opposite bank:

'Sam!'

'Sir?' said Mr. Weller.

'Here, I want you.'

'Let go, sir,' said Sam. 'Don't you hear the governor a-callin'? Let go, sir.'

With a violent effort, Mr. Weller disengaged himself from the grasp of the agonized Pickwickian, and in so doing administered a considerable impetus to the unhappy Mr. Winkle. With an accuracy which no degree of dexterity or practice could have insured, that unfortunate gentleman bore swiftly down into the centre of the reel, at the very moment when Mr. Bob Sawyer was performing a flourish of unparalleled beauty. Mr. Winkle struck wildly against him, and with a loud crash they both fell heavily down. Mr. Pickwick ran to the spot. Bob Sawyer had risen to his feet, but Mr. Winkle was far too wise to do anything of the kind, in skates. He was seated on the ice making spasmodic efforts to smile; but anguish was depicted on every lineament of his countenance.

WINTER

ALFRED LORD TENNYSON

The frost is here,
The fuel is dear,
And woods are sear,
And fires burn clear,
And frost is here
And has bitten the heel of the going year.

Bite, frost, bite!
You roll up away from the light,
The blue wood-louse, and the plump
dormouse,
And the bees are stilled, and the flies are
killed,
And you bite far into the heart of the
house,
But not into mine.

Bite, frost, bite!
The woods are all the searer,
The fuel is all the dearer,
The fires are all the clearer,
My spring is all the nearer,
You have bitten into the heart of the earth,
But not into mine.